... WHAT'S AT ISSUE? ....

www.heinemann.co.uk/library
Visit our website to find out more information about **Heinemann Library** books.

To order:
☎ Phone 44 (0) 1865 888066
 Send a fax to 44 (0) 1865 314091
🖥 Visit the Heinemann Bookshop at www.heinemann.co.uk/library to browse our catalogue and order online.

First published in Great Britain by Heinemann Library, Halley Court, Jordan Hill, Oxford OX2 8EJ, a division of Reed Educational and Professional Publishing Ltd. Heinemann is a registered trademark of Reed Educational & Professional Publishing Limited.

OXFORD MELBOURNE AUCKLAND JOHANNESBURG BLANTYRE
GABORONE IBADAN PORTSMOUTH NH (USA) CHICAGO

Designed by Tinstar Design (www.tinstar.co.uk)
Illustrations by Nicholas Beresford-Davies
Originated by Ambassador Litho Ltd
Printed in Hong Kong/China

ISBN 0 431 03559 8   (hardback)   ISBN 0 431 03567 9   (paperback)
06 05 04 03 02   06 05 04 03 02
10 9 8 7 6 5 4 3 2   10 9 8 7 6 5 4 3 2 1

British Library Cataloguing in Publication Data
Wignall, Paul
        Human Rights. – (What's at issue?)
        1. Human Rights – Juvenile literature
        I. Title
        323

Acknowledgements
The Publishers would like to thank the following for permission to reproduce photographs:
AKG: pp5, 7; Amnesty International: p17, p30; Bubbles: Pauline Cutles p23; Corbis: pp8, 9, Hulton-Deutsch pp4, 26, Bettmann pp6, 20, 34, David Muench p11, Monika Smith p12, Flip Schulke p21, Owen Franken p22, AFP p27, Pablo Corral Vega p31, David S Robbins p39; Cumulus: Gareth Boden: p35; John Walmsley: p41; Kobal Collection: p18; Photodisc: p36-37; Popperfoto: p25; UNESCO: pp28, 32; United Nations: p38.

Cover photograph: Nils Jorgensen.

Our thanks to Julie Turner (Head of Student Services and SENCO, Banbury School, Oxfordshire) for her comments in the preparation of this book.

Every effort has been made to contact copyright holders of any material reproduced in this book. Any omissions will be rectified in subsequent printings if notice is given to the Publisher.

Any words appearing in the text in bold, **like this**, are explained in the Glossary.

Contents

Introduction

How can people live together happily? How do we respect one another and treat each other fairly? Does everyone have a right to be treated the same as everybody else? Or is it always the case that some people will be more powerful, or richer, or better educated than others? These are some of the most important questions we can ever ask, and many people spend their whole lives trying to answer them. We hope that this book will help you begin to answer them for yourself.

A tale of two cities

Human beings have always lived in groups. Because of this we are often described as social animals. Early human beings lived in small groups, hunting for their food. As they became more settled, they learned to grow crops and care for animals, providing them with food. Gradually these settlements grew as groups of families lived close together for protection, to share food and to share their skills in making things. And so, villages, towns and cities grew up. Of course, even the biggest cities were a lot smaller than modern towns, but many of the problems we are faced with today were already beginning to appear, as the following story shows.

Tyrannopolis and Demopolis

Once upon a time on the shore of a great sea, there were two cities. Situated under the shadow of the same range of mountains, they were only a day's journey apart, but in every other way they were totally different. On a high hill in the centre of **Tyrannopolis** (which means, 'the city of the king') was a magnificent palace where the city's ruler lived. He was the richest man in the city, because everyone else who lived there brought him all the things they made, all the fish they caught in the sea and all the crops and livestock from their farms. He stored it in huge warehouses and gave back to the people just enough to live on while he sold the rest to traders who came from far away.

Tyrannopolis? History is full of **tyrants** like Adolf Hitler.

One day a trader, who was writing a book about the cities she visited, asked the king to describe Tyrannopolis and this is what he said: 'I am the king. The city is mine and no one else can tell me what to do. Everyone else here is a slave. They give me all I need and in return I feed them and protect them. But Tyrannopolis is mine and when I die it will be my son's.'

The trader sailed one day's journey down the coast and came to **Demopolis** (which means 'city of the people'). There was no palace there, but a number of fine houses. She asked to meet the king but was told they had no king. Every week the people of Demopolis met to discuss their plans and decide what to do. Each year someone was elected as their 'president', to organize the city's life and

Demopolis? Athens is often seen as the first democracy, but in fact most of its inhabitants were slaves.

carry out the decisions they had all made. The trader met this year's president, who said: 'The city belongs to all the people who live here. The decisions we make are for the good of everybody. We have to look after one another so that we are all safe and we can all prosper. We don't always get it right, but we do our best.'

Which of these two cities would you prefer to live in? Would you rather be the ruler of Tyrannopolis, or the president of Demopolis? Do you think the cities could learn anything from each other?

The Great Charter

From the earliest times people have debated over the organization of their society. There are those who believe a few people have the right to rule over others, with the majority simply there to meet the needs of the few who rule, and those who think that all human beings should be treated with respect, dignity and equality, and that it is the job of rulers to make sure this happens.

Magna Carta

In 1215, the king of England, King John, faced a rebellion from some of his **barons**. They were no longer prepared to accept what they saw as the misuse of royal power. On 15 June of that year, at Runnymede, an island in the river Thames, the king signed the **Magna Carta** (the Latin words mean 'Great Charter') in which he accepted a set of demands limiting his power. These included agreements that no one should be imprisoned without trial according to the law of the land, that citizens should be allowed to own and inherit property, and that all proposals by the king to raise money by taxation should be approved by the Great Council or Parliament before they took effect. The Magna Carta was an important step in establishing the idea of equality under the rule of law; from now on, in principle at least, English rulers were required to abide by the law of the land, and those laws would be decided by the ruler in agreement with a wider group of people.

The Magna Carta was the first attempt to limit the powers of the English king and to give everyone the protection of law.

MAGNA CARTA
Regis Johannis.

After defeat in the Civil War, King Charles I was executed in 1649.

The EXECUTION of KING CHARLES the FIRST, before the Banqueting House Whitehall, January 30.1648-9.

The growth of Parliament

At first this wider group of people were themselves more powerful than most – they were rich landowners, looking after their own interests – but the Magna Carta encouraged the idea that all people should have basic rights to equal treatment, and that one of the duties of government is to protect those rights. Over several hundred years Parliament came to represent more sections of society, and **merchants** and smaller landowners began to influence the making of law. In 1642 the struggle for power between ruler and Parliament turned into open war. Parliament's army defeated King Charles I, and he was tried and executed in 1649. Rule by Parliament alone lasted for another 13 years before Charles' son, Charles II, became king of England, but the overriding power of the single ruler in Britain had gone for ever. In 1688 Parliament **deposed** another king, James II, and invited Prince William of Orange, a Dutchman, to be king instead. From now on there was to be a balance of power between ruler and Parliament.

Natural rights

In the 18th century, ideas about human nature began to change. European explorers began to come home with tales of other peoples – in Asia, Africa and the Pacific – who seemed to live with natural freedom and happiness. Some thinkers, especially in France, contrasted these stories with their own experiences of being controlled by government and came to the conclusion that we all once lived in this state of natural freedom. They argued that everyone has the same understanding of right and wrong which is only corrupted by living in society. They also came to believe that because all men (but not at that time women) share the same natural capacity for freedom and happiness, then it is possible to **reform** society to allow these natural characteristics to flourish. They argued that human rights are things we all share because we are human beings.

Rousseau and revolution

An 18th century French thinker, Jean-Jacques Rousseau (1712–1778), said that although we are born free, society puts us in chains. These chains begin to be made as soon as we introduce the idea of private property: 'The man who first had the idea of enclosing a field and saying "This is mine", and found people foolish enough to believe him, was the real founder of society.' Rousseau wanted European society to be like the imaginary worlds of the travellers' tales, where freedom from control would lead to happier and simpler lives.

The American Declaration of Independence states that all men are equal.

Rousseau's ideas influenced political movements later in the 18th century. In 1776, British colonies in North America proclaimed their independence from Britain in their Declaration of Independence, and in 1789, elected representatives of the people of France set up the first French **republic**, executing the king three years later.

DECLARATIONS

The United States Declaration of Independence begins: 'We hold these truths to be self-evident; that all men are created equal, that they are endowed by their creator with certain… rights, that among these are life, liberty and the pursuit of happiness'; while the French 'Declaration of the Rights of Man and of the Citizen' announced 'all men are born free and equal in rights'.

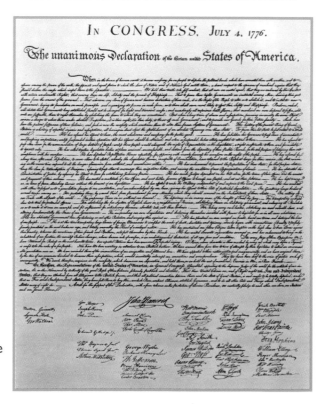

Some were not hopeful about the aims of these two revolutions. The Englishman Edmund Burke said that far from humans being corrupted by living in society, they need a stable social world in which to live and grow. Burke accepted that the conditions in which many people lived were unacceptable and needed to be changed. But he argued that the French revolutionaries had actually destroyed any long-term chance of improvement for ordinary people. For Burke, human rights were best safeguarded by a 'balance of power' in which no one group of people could easily dominate another.

The Rights of Man

One of the most influential books of this period was written by Thomas Paine, an Englishman who moved to live in North America. He wrote *The Rights of Man* in 1791 as a reply to Edmund Burke. Paine thought that when Burke said people 'look up with awe to kings; with duty to magistrates; with respect to nobility' and that this provides a proper balance in society, he had simply missed the point that these kings, magistrates and nobles were the **oppressors** of ordinary people. Paine argued that 'despotism' – rule by unquestioned authority – trickles down through the whole of society: despotic kings lead to despotic parents, creating a society that is in a permanent state of war within itself. Human rights, for Paine, are about the freedom and dignity of individuals to be themselves, and to be able to share in decision-making. He thought that everyone, if properly educated and encouraged, could take a responsible role in government, which would in turn help them to live in freedom, dignity, self-respect and peace. Paine's book was translated into many languages and became a powerful force for change in many countries.

People in the 18th century began to ask basic questions about how people should live together. Who do you agree with – Jacques Rousseau, Thomas Paine or Edmund Burke?

Thomas Paine – an Englishman who moved to America, and whose book, *The Rights of Man*, inspired revolutions in many countries.

Rights or happiness?

During the 19th century ideas about human rights began to change. As Europeans began to learn more about other cultures they realized that the old ideas of natural freedom were based on a misunderstanding. People in Asia, Africa or the sunny South Sea Islands were as troubled about what was right and what was wrong as were people in Britain or France. They also saw that it was impossible to find any two societies that shared the same set of beliefs about right and wrong or about justice. Finally, societies were becoming increasingly complicated: cities were growing, industry and trade was expanding, and the gap between rich and poor was getting wider.

While the old idea of 'natural rights' – things we share just because we were human, and which the government must allow to flourish – was collapsing, new ideas were beginning to replace it.

An English thinker, Jeremy Bentham (1748–1832), believed that: 'It is the greatest happiness of the greatest number that is the measure of right and wrong.' He did not think there were any 'natural rights', but that our duty to treat people equally and with respect was based on our duty to bring about as much happiness in the world as possible. John Stuart Mill (1806–1873) was a follower of Bentham who saw that the way we live with others requires striking a balance between what is right for ourselves and what is right for others. For instance, to take a modern example, how do we balance one person's right to smoke if they want to with the rights of a non-smoker to have a healthier, smoke-free environment, and not to help pay the cost of the medical care the smoker is more likely to need?

Mill realized that for individuals to be truly happy, society must leave them at least some areas where they can be themselves, and not controlled by others. But are there limits to freedom? Can you be free to drive on the wrong side of the road or take anything you need from a supermarket without paying for it? How might your freedom affect other people?

Henry Thoreau

Writing in America at the same time, Henry Thoreau (1817–1862), a great believer in personal freedom, and the first person to use the actual phrase 'human rights', said: 'that government governs best which governs least'. He went on to argue that the job of a government is 'to protect the individual's freedom – his right to live in the manner he chooses without interference from others.' As to our own obligations, Thoreau said 'the only obligation which I have a right to assume, is to do at any time what I think right.' This is not about being selfish, but does lead on to the idea that, if I think that a government is not meeting its obligation to protect the freedom and dignity of everyone in society, then I have a right to protest.

Thoreau's arguments were of great importance in the 20th century, inspiring Mahatma Gandhi's and Martin Luther King's non-violent opposition to political **oppression** in India and the United States, for example, while giving courage to many individuals to stand up for what they believe to be right.

Walden Pond near Concord, Massachusetts, USA. Thoreau lived alone here from July 1845 to September 1847, in order 'to live deliberately, to front only the essential facts of life'. One of these 'facts' was the importance of human rights.

Universal rights

The second half of the 19th century was a time when many issues that we now think of as 'human rights' issues began to arise. Although anti-slavery campaigns started as early as 1688 in the United States, a **civil war** was fought between 1861 and 1865 between those who wanted slavery to be outlawed and those who wanted it to continue. At the same time, **reformers** throughout Europe and America attacked other types of injustice allowed by law – the use of child labour, brutal working practices, starvation wages and appalling conditions in towns and factories. The rights of women and children and of **ethnic minorities** to equal and dignified treatment began to be fought for, both by violent and non-violent means.

Modern context

In the 20th century, as governments got more powerful, and sometimes **abused** that power, so the demands for **equality of opportunity**, fair treatment and freedom grew. The idea that a nation was a place where just one recognizable group of people lived – with a shared language and history – led to minorities within nations being **persecuted**. In Germany in the 1930s, attacks on Jews became more and more vicious, and then the ruling Nazi party began to transport them to concentration camps where they were systematically killed, along with Gypsies (people who live as travellers), homosexuals (people attracted to members of the same sex) and other groups who had done nothing other than be 'different'. In many other countries, too, minority groups were ill-treated and given few political or **civil rights**.

The United Nations building, in New York, USA. It is the headquarters of the General Assembly of the United Nations, which today represents 188 member states (countries or independent states).

As international communications improved, such human rights issues could be set in a wider context. No longer were abuses of power, and the denial of justice, equality and dignity to individuals and groups just local concerns. They could affect the whole world and groups in one country could put pressure on other governments to change.

At the end of the Second World War, and with the founding of the **United Nations** (UN), a Universal Declaration of Human Rights was drawn up and published on 10 December 1948. The UN Declaration was one of the most important human rights documents in the 20th century.

HUMAN RIGHTS FILMS

Three films on human rights are:

- *Gandhi*, the story of the growth of 'non-violent protest' in India
- *Cry Freedom*, an account of civil rights protest in South Africa
- *Schindler's List*, a moving story of a man risking his life to save Jews from death during the Second World War.

There are also a number of film production companies and film festivals throughout the world that are dedicated to making and showing films about human rights.

UNIVERSAL DECLARATION OF HUMAN RIGHTS

The Preamble (introduction) to the UN Declaration states that:

- recognition of the inherent dignity and of the equal rights of all members of the human family is the foundation of freedom, justice and peace in the world…
- disregard and contempt for human rights have resulted in **barbarous** acts which have outraged the conscience of mankind…
- it is essential… that human rights should be protected by the rule of law…
- the peoples of the United Nations have… reaffirmed their faith in fundamental human rights, in the dignity and worth of the human person and in the equal rights of men and women and have determined to promote social progress and better standards of life in larger freedom…
- have pledged themselves to achieve… the promotion of universal respect for and observance of human rights and fundamental freedoms…

While Articles 1 and 2 state that:

- All human beings are born free and equal in dignity and rights. They are endowed with reason and conscience and should act towards one another in a spirit of brotherhood.
- Everyone is entitled to all the rights and freedoms set forth in this Declaration without distinction of any kind, such as race, colour, sex, language, religion, political or other opinion, national or social origin, property, birth or other status.

Rights and responsibilities

The history of human rights began with limited demands for equal treatment in law, but over the centuries these have widened, as attempts have been made to limit the power of rulers, and demands for all people to be treated fairly, with dignity and without fear, have become increasingly common.

Some people think that there is no such thing as human rights. They argue that people are so different at different times and in different places that it would be impossible for them to agree on what is right and what is wrong. Imagine one of the **barons** who forced King John to sign the **Magna Carta** in 1215 sitting down with Thomas Paine or with the present **secretary-general** of the **United Nations**. They would have very different views about human freedom and dignity, and the baron would not even know what the term 'human rights' means. Many people who don't believe in equal human rights probably still want everyone to be as happy and free from suffering as possible.

Needs of the many

The British thinker Alasdair MacIntyre, in his book *After Virtue* (1981), says that the idea of human rights is such a recent one – little more than 200 years old – that it can hardly be seen as a fundamental part of being human. He thinks we should think of men and women not so much as separate individuals but as part of wider groups – families, schools, nations, and so on. What we have, he argues, is not so much a right to be ourselves, as a responsibility to live properly with other people. The decisions an individual takes should not be so much about what's good for 'me', but rather what's good for 'us'. If it is good for us, then it will probably be good enough for me.

But what happens when rules about right and wrong get twisted to meet the needs not of the many but only of the few? Ideas of human rights grew up just at the moment when people felt that their freedom and dignity – and that of other people – was being destroyed by selfish rulers. Imagine a school class getting along quite well, having agreed rules for responsible behaviour, and then the students who sit nearest the windows suddenly decide they want to make everyone else pay for the light and air coming into the room. Those furthest away from the windows might well start to complain, and it is likely that they would say things like, 'we all have a right to this light and air'.

Balancing act

Perhaps the idea of human rights grows when we can no longer agree about what is responsible behaviour, and the inequalities between groups of people become intolerable. Does the late arrival of human rights ideas into history mean that the ideas are not very important, or does it mean we have grown to be more aware of the complex balance between individual freedom and dignity and the responsibilities we all share when we live together?

Can you think of other examples where rights and responsibilities have to be balanced? Are there times when rights are more important than responsibilities, or the other way round?

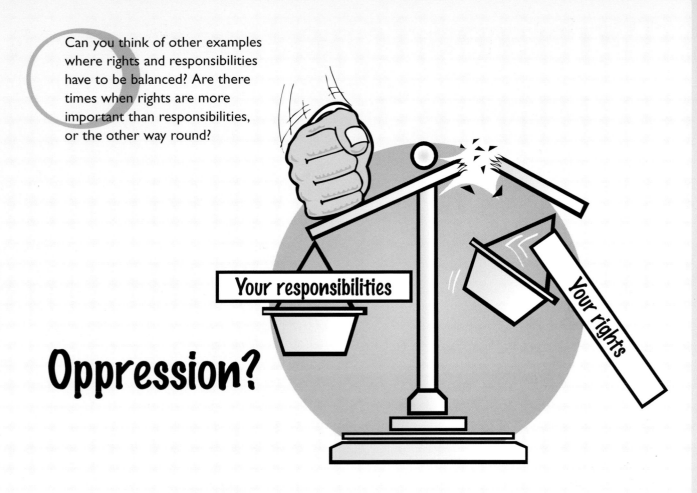

Your responsibilities

Your rights

Oppression?

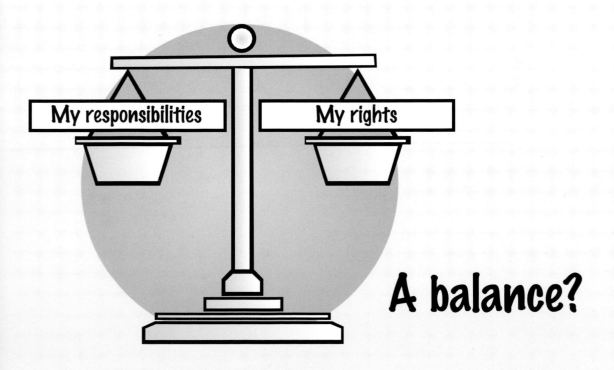

My responsibilities

My rights

A balance?

Rights and the law

The Universal Declaration of Human Rights says that it is a human right to be protected by the law from torture (Article 5), from detention or arrest without good reason (Article 9) and to have a fair hearing in court (Articles 10 and 11). In Britain, the rights of people suspected of committing a crime are stated in the Police and Criminal Evidence Act, 1984 (usually referred to as PACE). This act gives the police powers to stop and search people or vehicles if they have a 'reasonable suspicion' that a crime has been committed, or someone intends to commit a crime. What is reasonable here is for a court of law to decide, and if a court decides that the police have no reasonable grounds for stopping and searching, they can dismiss the prosecution.

PACE allows the police to stop and search you for offensive weapons or for something made to be used in a crime. There are many rules about how searches can take place, all of which are intended to protect you from unnecessary embarrassment or intimidation. The police can also search homes and other places, either with the consent of the owner or if they have been granted a search warrant by a magistrate. Some things are excluded from searches – for example, medical records or possibly school records – but the courts may require these things to be produced later on.

There are many offences for which the police can arrest a suspect. In some situations a member of the public can arrest someone if they see them committing an offence (this is usually called a 'citizen's arrest'). However, the police do not encourage anyone to do this if they risk getting hurt in the process, and recommend letting the suspect go if there is any danger.

FACT

● *In 1998 the police and security forces of 125 countries were known to be torturing prisoners. This number had risen to 132 countries in 1999.*

CASE STUDY

Andrey Klimov, a member of the Belarusian parliament, was arrested after protesting against the president. He was charged with misusing official money, but many people believe this was a charge invented to justify putting him in prison. Klimov was on trial for eight months, during which time he had to be taken to hospital after being beaten up by prison guards, and brought into court wearing no shoes and with his clothes torn. On 17 March 2000 he was found guilty of 'building without a permit' and sentenced to six years in prison.

Klimov has always said he was innocent and he is one of a number of Belarusians arrested after criticizing the president. Others include a former Prime Minister, Mikhail Chigir, and another MP, Valery Kudinov.

This 35-year-old man from Kuwait was arrested in 1991, then beaten with electric cable and burned with cigarettes while in custody.

Once arrested, a suspect cannot be held without charge for more than 96 hours (and usually for only 24 hours), and must be given access to a **solicitor** to help them. Young people can only be interviewed when a 'responsible adult' – a parent, guardian or sometimes a **social worker** – is present. All suspects have a right not to say anything, and to take notes about what is happening. The police must give suspects materials to use for these notes. Suspects also have the right to see a doctor and to have photographs taken if they believe they have been injured while being arrested or questioned.

In many countries, rights such as these are often ignored. People can be arrested for no reason, detained without charge, assaulted, tortured and even killed without any protection from the law.

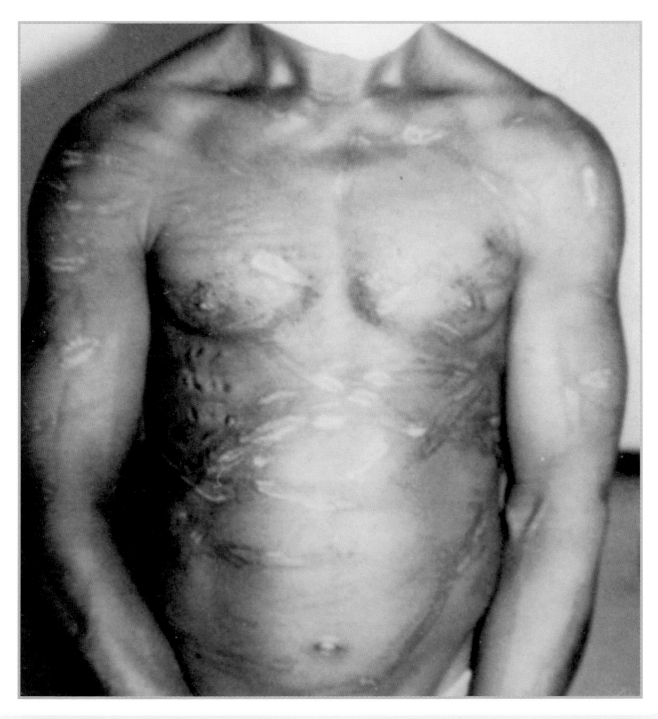

Information and privacy

Can we say what we like? The **United Nations**' Universal Declaration of Human Rights says that, 'everyone has the right to freedom of opinion and expression' (Article 19). But as the European Convention on Human Rights also says, 'the exercise of these freedoms… carries with it duties and responsibilities' (Article 10.2). When you say something about another person that isn't true, this is **slander**; and if you write it down, it becomes **libel**. But reasonable criticism is another matter, and we should be free to express our opinions, or raise doubts about something that has happened, without fear.

Whistleblowers

Sometimes, employees of companies, or of governments, may discover that those they are working with (and perhaps they themselves) are involved in illegal activities, or are being expected to cover up wrongdoing. What should they do? In 1984, a scientist discovered that equipment used by the police which he was involved in making was not accurate and could lead to wrongful convictions. He told a national newspaper who wanted to publish the story. However, the man's employers tried to prevent the information going in to the paper, saying that it was confidential. In the end, a

Karen Silkwood was mysteriously killed in an 'accident', just as she was about to reveal information about dangerous practices at a nuclear plant. A film was made of the story, starring Meryl Streep.

judge decided that it was not wrong for the newspaper to publish the story because it could prevent people being wrongly convicted of crimes.

What do I have a right to see?

People have the right to see any personal information about themselves (but not about other people) held on a computer or in other files. These include medical and social work records as well as school records. In England and Wales children and young people can apply to see their own records and parents or guardians can apply if the child has given consent, or is too young to understand (so long as it is in the child's interests for the parent to know). Parents have no absolute rights to see their child's records, although in Scotland parents do exercise this right if their child is under 16. If you want to see your file, you will usually do so with an official person present – to help you understand. There are some pieces of information which you may not be able to see, and officials can explain why this is the case. If you find mistakes about facts in your file, you can demand to have them put right.

The general principles are that information about us should be accurate, available for us to see, and helpful to other people who may (confidentially) need to have the information in order to help us. When this information is no longer needed, it should be destroyed.

In most circumstances you have the right to see information about yourself.

Medical Notes

School

Social Services

Housing Department

Civil rights

When the American Declaration of Independence declared in 1776 that 'all men are created equal', much of the wealth of the country depended on slave labour. It was not until the 1830s that a movement to abolish (do away with) slavery in the United States got seriously under way (although the slave trade had been abolished in Britain in 1807) and it was only in 1865 that slaves were finally freed. But the relationship between the white and black communities remained unequal. Most released slaves remained in the employment of white masters, for low wages and in poor conditions. Even in the northern states, which had been the first to abolish slavery, there were very few opportunities for real economic and social equality.

Civil rights demonstrators scuffle with the police in Newark, New Jersey, USA, on 3 July 1963.

This state of affairs continued throughout the first half of the 20th century. Many southern states had segregation laws, keeping white and black people apart. One law, in Montgomery, Alabama, prohibited black people from sitting next to whites on a bus. On 1 December 1955, Mrs Rosa Parks, a black woman, was arrested when she refused to stand to let a white man take her seat. As she said later, it wasn't that she was tired, she was just tired of giving in. Rosa Parks' action was the beginning of a massive **campaign** of protest and civil disobedience which gradually led to the repeal of the segregation laws.

The most famous leader of this **civil rights** movement was Martin Luther King, a black clergyman. In 1963, he led a protest meeting in Washington DC, the capital city of the United States, attended by 250,000 people. In his speech to the meeting he reminded Americans of their earliest commitment to human rights: 'So I say to you, my friends, that even though we must face the difficulties of today and tomorrow, I still have a dream. It is a dream deeply rooted in the American dream that one day this nation will rise up and live out the true meaning of its creed – we hold these truths to be self-evident, that all men are created equal.'

King was murdered in 1968, but the civil rights movement he inspired has continued to grow, and to inspire other groups in other countries. Civil rights – the demand that different racial or ethnic communities living together should meet on equal terms under the law, share the same opportunities and be treated with the same respect – remains one of the most difficult of human rights to obtain and to keep.

Martin Luther King was the inspirational leader of the civil rights movement, who was murdered for his beliefs in 1968.

FACTS

Important dates for the abolition of slavery:
- *1807 – United Kingdom abolishes the slave trade in its Empire;*
- *1835 – United Kingdom abolishes the keeping of slaves in its Empire;*
- *1865 – the United States abolishes slavery.*

Racial equality

The **United Nations'** Universal Declaration says that human rights apply to everyone 'without distinction of any kind, such as race, colour… religion… national or social origin' (Article 2). The British Race Relations Act (1976), which also set up the Commission for Racial Equality (CRE), deals with **discrimination** in England, Wales and Scotland.

Race Relations Act

The Race Relations Act identifies three kinds of discrimination: direct discrimination, indirect discrimination, and victimization. Direct discrimination happens when someone treats one person less favourably than they would another because of their race. For example, a shop which said, 'no blacks served here' would be guilty of direct discrimination, and so would an employer who refused to give someone

Today, white and black communities live together in Britain with greater co-operation and tolerance than in the past.

a job 'because the customers would stay away'. The second type of discrimination – indirect discrimination – takes place when a group or individual is put at a disadvantage. For example, an employer who said they would only take on clean-shaven staff may be indirectly discriminating against Sikh men, who generally have beards because of their religious beliefs. Finally, victimization occurs when a person treats someone else badly to get back at them for having done something they don't like. For example, it would be victimization if an employer sacked a black employee who has made a complaint about the employer's discrimination.

Although there are some exceptions, for instance it is lawful to employ only Chinese waiters in a Chinese restaurant, most employment is now controlled by the Race Relations Act, as is education and training. For example, no school can refuse to take pupils, or exclude them, on the grounds of race.

The Commission for Racial Equality (CRE)

The CRE is responsible for helping British society work towards eliminating all racial discrimination. It will investigate complaints about racial discrimination and may bring people to court. All local authorities, such as housing departments and **social services**, also have a duty both to eliminate unlawful racial discrimination and to promote **equality of opportunity** for people from all racial groups.

Sometimes individuals or groups try to stir up racial hatred. Any public attempts to insult or inflame attitudes to other racial groups can lead to prosecution under the Public Order Act 1986, which also makes it an offence to possess any threatening, abusive or insulting literature in order to stir up racial hatred. Placing such material on the internet or downloading it may also be an offence.

It is against the law to refuse to admit anyone to a school because of their race.

APARTHEID

The practice of keeping racial groups separate is sometimes called segregation, and sometimes **apartheid**. Apartheid is an **Afrikaans** word meaning 'separateness' and became a basis of law in South Africa for many years. South Africans were divided into the categories of 'white', 'coloured' and 'black', and strict rules dictated where different groups could live, what jobs they could do, and where and how they could travel or be educated. A largely non-violent protest movement – supported by many other countries, which refused to trade with South Africa – eventually brought an end to apartheid. One leader of the black community, Nelson Mandela, was released after 26 years of imprisonment, and he became South Africa's first black president. Mandela's aim was a non-racial democracy to enable all the communities to live together in his country. Bishop Desmond Tutu coined the phrase 'rainbow people' to replace the old idea of separation. South Africa still has many economic and social difficulties, and, just as in the United States, old social patterns will take a long time to overcome, but it has begun to move away from apartheid with remarkably little violence.

Anti-Semitism and ethnic cleansing

Anti-Semitism

Anti-Semitism is a very old but persistent attitude that involves deliberate **discrimination** against, or **persecution** of, Jewish people. It is a conscious attempt to deny Jewish people their right to equal treatment, and has involved putting them inside social and actual boundaries (ghettos), taking away their dignity, and justifying this ill-treatment by claiming that Jews are the enemies of any state in which they live.

From 1933 to 1939, German Jews were systematically and deliberately discriminated against, **oppressed** and eventually **repressed** by being put outside the protection of the law. During those years 'Jews not wanted here' signs were put up in cafes, shops and at the entrance to towns and villages. In October 1933, Jewish doctors were banned from hospitals. In September 1935, Jews were officially named 'second class citizens' and in November 1938, German schools were closed to Jewish children. All Jews were also made to wear a yellow '**Star of David**' badge on their clothing. From 1939 to 1945, as Adolf Hitler's Germany dominated much of Europe, this repression turned into a programme of killing. During this period, almost 6 million Jews died, while about 800,000 others escaped to countries outside German influence.

The power of this prejudice continues, however. Neo-Nazi groups (modern supporters of Hitler's views) are still strong in Germany and elsewhere in Europe, particularly where there are economic problems which can be 'blamed' on **immigration**. Many groups other than Jews have been targeted in this way at different times. **Ethnic minorities**, women, and the gay and lesbian community, for example, have had to suffer the effects of fear and anxiety about differences, and been the object of hatred, ill-treatment and even death, simply because they were different from the powerful majority.

Modern conflicts and ethnic cleansing

After the Second World War, many Jews were vulnerable because they had no land of their own. The land of Israel became their homeland, but this involved displacing Palestinian Arabs already living there. Jews and Palestinians have not found it easy to live together.

The Kurds are another people with no homeland. There are 22 million Kurds, most of whom are Muslims (followers of the Islamic religion). They live in parts of Turkey, Iraq, Iran and Syria. Their rights have been ignored by those governments, who have persecuted and at times systematically killed them.

Peoples sharing a homeland with others can be very vulnerable. The conflict in the Balkans during the 1990s brought the phrase 'ethnic cleansing' into popular use. Ethnic cleansing is the systematic attempt by one national or religious group to use force to expel another group from the area in which they live. So, in the Balkan states of Serbia, Croatia, and then Kosovo, minority groups were attacked and forced to leave their homes, and many of the men were killed. After attacks on Kosovan Albanians by the Serbian army, western nations led by the USA and Britain used force to help protect them.

In 1948, the sub-continent of India was divided into two countries: India and Pakistan. There was fierce fighting on the borders. These **refugees** from Kashmir are typical of refugees anywhere at any time – tired, hungry and afraid.

Immigration, refugees and asylum

In June 1948, an old troopship, the *Empire Windrush*, sailed into the port of London with 510 people from the West Indies on board. They were not allowed to land at first. Initially they were housed in a large air-raid shelter on Clapham Common, then moved into houses in Brixton. This became the core of the Afro-Caribbean community in Britain. **Immigration** from the West Indies, and later from India and Pakistan, was encouraged by the government, and the numbers of immigrants grew. Around 60,000 immigrants arrived in 1960, and 120,000 in 1961. Communities developed in many towns and cities – especially St Paul's in Bristol, Brixton and Southall in London, Manningham in Bradford, and the inner-Leeds area.

Although the 1976 Race Relations Act made it illegal to discriminate against someone because of their colour, race, nationality, national or **ethnic** origin, black communities point out that they experience **discrimination** every day of their lives. It is a part of their British experience. The main function of black communities for Britain had been to provide a cheap work force. But black communities have often felt that they don't have the same access to employment, housing, health care or education as white communities. Black people are more likely to be arrested on suspicion of being involved in crime, and find it harder to get a job.

Refugees and asylum seekers

Not everyone who leaves the country of their birth to live somewhere else does so for economic reasons. Some are **refuges** – they leave because they are being persecuted and are afraid that if they stay they will be killed or put in prison. Many Jews left Germany and Eastern Europe in the 1930s to escape Nazi **persecution**. The break-up of Yugoslavia in the 1990s has led to many people from Bosnia and Kosovo, for example, trying to escape to other countries.

These two Jewish children are returning to Germany in 1939, having been refused entry into America. What did the future hold for them?

In November 1998, about 31,000 people from what had once been Yugoslavia asked for permission to live in another European country. Between January and March 2000, the number had fallen to 11,600. However, they were still the largest group of **asylum seekers**, followed by people from Iraq (7060), Afghanistan (5910) and Turkey (5250). People seek asylum (a safe place to live) because they are afraid to remain in their own country – perhaps because their basic human rights to speak out against their own government, or to practise their own religion, are forbidden. But they are not necessarily made welcome in their new countries. They may find it difficult to earn money – especially if they are not able to speak the country's language. Although the numbers of asylum seekers are actually quite small, they can seem threatening to other countries.

How do you think we should treat people escaping from another country? Does it make a difference whether they want to settle permanently in their new home, or go back to their birth country? How do

These children were among thousands of Kosovans who fled from the war in their country during 1998 and 1999.

we help people live with dignity when they have lost their homes, and often their families, and are afraid to return to a place where they may be killed or put in prison? What would you do?

ASYLUM IN THE UK

People in the United Kingdom sometimes say that the country has 'more than its fair share' of asylum seekers, and others think that most people seeking asylum are doing so under false pretences. But figures show that most of the many people escaping war and persecution stay in a country very close to their own, and that right across Europe, the United Kingdom is only ninth in the list of countries where people seek a place of safety. Again, the government's own figures show that in the majority of cases, asylum seekers remain in the United Kingdom because it is accepted that they would be in danger of death or persecution if they returned to their own country.

27

International human rights

The earliest expression of what we now think of as human rights was the **Magna Carta**. By the 18th century some people began to think that all men (but not at that stage women) shared some rights. These 'universal rights' crossed the boundaries of countries. But how far should one country interfere in the laws and practices of another? Human rights may cross frontiers, but is it acceptable for one country to force these rights on another? What do you think?

International action

Nations are sometimes able to agree on international laws and codes of conduct. For example, the Geneva Convention of 1949 is an international agreement on the conduct of war – the care of wounded and captured soldiers, for instance – while more recently the discovery of a hole in the ozone layer over the Antarctic has led to attempts to limit the emission of gases that may be damaging the atmosphere. In human rights, however, there is often a reluctance on the part of one government to interfere with another. Governments may talk about human rights, but often fail to take action. Countries trade with one another, for instance, and if one country is critical of another's human rights record, it may harm their trading relationship. And as nearly all countries have some human rights failings, there is always the fear that criticism could lead to their own record being exposed to the public view.

What level of intervention should exist between countries?

Sometimes, however, the scale of human rights **abuse** is so great that international action is taken. During the Second World War, there was an agreement made to put accused Germans to trial in the countries where their crimes were committed. Of course, for the leaders of the Nazi movement that was not realistic. An international tribunal was set up consisting of four members – Britain, USA,

France and Russia. The trials, lasting from November 1945 to October 1946, became known as the Nuremberg Trials.

The white South African policy of **apartheid** began in 1948 when the Afrikaner-dominated National Party, came to power in the parliamentary elections. Increasingly divisive racial policies were put in place denying blacks basic civil liberties and rights. The African National Congress (ANC) and other opposition groups established the Freedom Charter calling for equal political rights for all races. An international trade boycott (whereby a number of countries refused to buy goods made in South Africa) followed in the mid-1980s that eventually contributed to the fall of apartheid.

INTERNATIONALLY RECOGNIZED HUMAN RIGHTS

Access to legal remedies for violations of rights

A social and international order to realize rights

Education

Equality of rights without discrimination

Equal protection of the law

Freedom of:
- movement and residence
- opinion, expression and the press
- thought, conscience and religion

Food, clothing and housing

Free trade unions

Health care

Humane treatment when detained or in prison

Liberty of person

Life

Marry and start a family

Nationality

Own property

Participation in cultural life

Political participation

Recognition as a person before the law

Security of person

Presumption of innocence

Protection against:
- advocacy of racial or religious hatred
- **arbitrary** arrest or detention
- arbitrary expulsion
- cruel and inhuman punishment
- imprisonment for debt
- torture

Protection from slavery

Protection of:
- minority cultures
- privacy, family and home

Rest and leisure

Seek asylum from persecution

Self-determination

Social security

Social services

Special protection for children

Work, under favourable conditions

Amnesty International

During the second half of the 20th century, many groups and organizations were set up to work for human rights of all kinds in their own countries, and many of them were able to bring about real changes in conditions for workers, women, children, prisoners, and so on. But as the century went on, it was clear that for many reasons much more international action was needed. For instance, nations were in close contact with others, through trade and **diplomacy**. The growth of **multi-national corporations** meant that working policies and practices might affect people in a number of countries at the same time. The expansion of the **media** allowed information to be spread across the world very quickly.

On May 28 1961, a British Sunday newspaper, *The Observer*, published an 'Appeal for Amnesty' on behalf of six 'prisoners of conscience' from different countries. These were people who had been imprisoned for the beliefs they held, not for committing any crime. The article asked people to write a letter to the governments of the countries in which the prisoners were held, making an appeal on behalf of these prisoners and any others who were in prison for their beliefs. This was the beginning of Amnesty International, and it was also the beginning of a new phase in human rights. The appeals were not necessarily to be made by people who shared the

Amnesty International have been fighting for human rights since 1961.

prisoners' beliefs; they were to be made because of a deeper belief that everyone should be allowed to speak freely, and think as their conscience dictates.

As Amnesty International grew, its work spread throughout the world. It works for the release of prisoners of conscience who have not used or encouraged the use of violence, and for fair trials for all people accused of committing crimes. It opposes torture and the use of the death penalty. It works for many groups denied human rights – not just prisoners, but also refugees.

Watch groups

Some people find Amnesty International's approach – though it is valuable and often successful – too limited. Human Rights Watch groups were formed to examine the record of governments and to publicize human rights **abuses** in different countries. These have included Helsinki Watch, formed in 1978 to monitor human rights in the former Soviet Union (though most of its members were immediately arrested), and groups in Chile (1973), East Timor (1975), Argentina (1976) and China (1979) – all countries that have denied people the right to speak freely in criticism of the government.

FACTS

During the second half of 1999:
- *there were allegations of torture and ill-treatment of prisoners in 27 European countries*
- *14 European countries imprisoned people for their political beliefs.*

ENEMY SPIES!

Amnesty International's ability to annoy governments can sometimes even be amusing. In 1977, the government of Argentina claimed that Amnesty was in fact working for the KGB, the Soviet Union's spy organization. At the same time the Soviet Union was complaining that Amnesty was working for the CIA, the United States' spy organization, and the main opponents of the KGB!

These women are holding pictures of men who 'disappeared' in Argentina because they opposed the **oppressive** military dictatorship.

FACT

- *In 1973 General Augusto Pinochet seized power in Chile. Between then and 1990, when some democracy returned, 2279 people, opponents of Pinochet's government, either 'disappeared' or were killed.*

Rights and choices

The late 20th century was a time of **globalization**: the spread of international **media** (television and the Internet especially), and trade and industry dominated by a small number of huge **multi-national corporations** (such as Microsoft, Sky television and Coca-Cola). Individual countries are affected by decisions made thousands of miles away by directors of companies. For example, the economy of a country depending on growing and selling bananas or oranges, may flourish or wither depending on the decision of a supermarket chain to sell that country's fruit in its supermarkets. On the other hand, individuals can choose to buy a car made in one of many different countries.

Globalization means that jobs and people, like these workers on a banana plantation, can be affected by decisions made in other countries.

At what cost?

This global economy, where decisions made in one place affect people thousands of miles away, is sometimes said to increase choice. But it also presents many challenges to the idea of human rights. A supermarket chain will want to buy fruit or vegetables as cheaply as possible, so they can sell them to their customers more cheaply than their competitors. Sometimes small nations or regions are encouraged to concentrate on the production of just one kind of food – bananas, for instance. Most of that country's agricultural land is turned over to this product, and it must rely on imports of other foods to feed its people. But what happens if there is a price war between supermarket chains in the rich countries? Then the buyers of bananas pay less to the producers and the farmers receive even less. This will mean that the countries that produce these items have to find ways of cutting their own costs, which may mean paying their workers less, perhaps even allowing children not to go to school and making them work for almost no wages.

However, Article 23 of the Universal Declaration of Human Rights says that 'Everyone has the right… to just and favourable remuneration [pay] ensuring for himself and his family an existence worthy of human dignity' while Article 32 of the Convention on the Rights of the Child (see pages 36–7) says that children have the right 'to be protected from economic **exploitation** and from performing any work that is likely… to interfere with the child's education, or to be harmful to the child's… development.'

A FAIR WAGE?

In his book *Hidden Agendas*, John Pilger reports a conversation with an 11-year-old Punjabi girl, Sonia, who has gone blind and earns her living stitching footballs. He asks her about the fun of being a child, but she says she has no fun because she has no choice. It takes her a day to stitch two footballs. For that day's work she is paid the equivalent of 15 pence. In the Punjab, 15 pence will not even buy one litre of milk. (You might like to find out how much a football costs in Britain. If the worker was paid 7.5 pence for making it, you might also like to ask yourself where the rest of the money you pay goes.)

The cost of the food you buy in a supermarket may be directly linked to human rights **abuses** elsewhere – although multi-national corporations do claim to be committed to human rights.

Trade frequently involves the abuse of human rights. The growth of sugar, tobacco, cotton and coffee plantations in the 18th century fuelled the slave trade. The competition to maximise profits by cutting the cost of production remains a key element in international trade. But how far does the sort of exploitation suffered by Sonia differ from the conditions in which slaves lived in the southern states of America at the beginning of the 19th century? What do you think you could do to change the way things are?

The rights of woman

Human rights began, to use Thomas Paine's phrase, as 'the Rights of Man' (1791). Women were not seen as having any rights of their own; they were legally bound to their father or their husband. In 1792, a radical thinker called Mary Wollstonecraft published *A Vindication of the Rights of Woman*, which boldly called for women to be treated as independent people, with their own rights, both in law and in everyday life. She was made fun of, but her views began to influence other women. During the 19th century more women were seen as independent people. Novelists, such as Charlotte and Emily Bronte and George Eliot (whose real name was Mary Ann Evans), and social **reformers**, such as Elizabeth Fry and Florence Nightingale, were famous and influential. Gradually, too, women demanded the right to vote in elections to Parliament, a right that had been granted to more men during the 19th century. Through the efforts of women such as Emmeline Pankhurst in Britain, they gained the vote in 1928. Women were also increasingly working as doctors and teachers, and the 20th century saw a growth in **equality of opportunity** in many countries, despite the efforts of some men (and even some women) to prevent it.

Inequality of relationship and of opportunity remains a fundamental part of many women's lives throughout the world. Many women are denied equal access with men to education or to jobs. Many women are paid less than men for the same work. Can you think of other areas of life where women are discriminated against?

Mary Wollstonecraft, author of *A Vindication of the Rights of Woman* (1792).

In 1979 the 'International Convention on the Elimination of all forms of **Discrimination** Against Women' was adopted by the UN, and in 1975 the Sex Discrimination Act (amended in 1986) laid out laws for the rights of men and women to equal treatment in Britain. The Sex Discrimination Act defines discrimination as direct and indirect. Direct discrimination is when someone is treated less favourably than someone of the opposite sex – for instance, not allowing a girl to do CDT (craft, design, technology) or a boy to do food technology in a school. Not allowing women to go into a pub, or not giving both men and women half-price drinks would also be classed as direct discrimination. Indirect discrimination is harder to define but it might include only allowing pupils who were studying PE to join an after-school football club, if most pupils studying PE were boys. This might indirectly discriminate against girls wanting to play football.

> The law, as well as good sense, accepts that men and women should have equality of opportunity. But there are no women in the Premier League – yet.

Arranged marriages

Article 16 of the Universal Declaration of Human Rights says that 'Marriage shall be entered into only with the free and full consent of the intending spouses.' In some cultures, young people have their marriages arranged for them by their families, and may never see their new husband or wife before the decision is taken for them. Many people accept this approach to marriage without question, and remain happily married, but for some it is a very unhappy situation. Do you think the Article is right? Or should cultures and families be able to decide for themselves? And what if your family, or someone whose family wants to make an arranged marriage, disagrees? How would you try to resolve a conflict like that?

Children's rights

Legally, anyone under the age of 18 is a child, although it's better to call older children 'young people'. The **United Nations** Convention on the Rights of the Child starts from the belief that children and young people need special protection because they can be very vulnerable, that all children and young people should be treated with the same care, and that anything that adults do for them or to them should be in the best interests of the children and young people themselves.

Lack of progress

Countries that agree to abide by the UN Convention should have laws which make sure that children will have proper health care and access to education, will be protected from work that is dangerous or that will prevent them from being healthy, and will be protected from **abuse** or **exploitation**, especially sexual exploitation or prostitution. Many countries do not have these laws, and of those that do, many ignore them or will not punish people who break them.

Every year the UN Committee on the Rights of the Child discusses the progress that has been made in protecting children's rights. At its meeting on 12 April 2000 the Commission heard that violations of children's rights had been alleged in 30 countries. At the same meeting a number of speakers said that children's rights were often talked about, but very little progress was being made in many countries to actually bring them about.

The UN Convention on the Rights of the Child says that the best place for children and young people to develop into confident adults is within their own families, and wants governments to do all they can to help families to meet this challenge.

THE UK'S FIRST REPORT TO THE U.N. COMMITTEE ON THE RIGHTS of the CHILD

The UK agrees to care for children as the UN Convention requires. This is the report written in 1994.

But sometimes families don't meet the needs of children. And sometimes governments, or employers, allow children and young people to be exploited. In many countries, children and young people may be protected by law from ill-treatment inside or outside their families, but what can be done where no such laws exist?

Many children's lives are a long way from the ideals of the UN Convention. These children are scavenging for rubbish in Manila in the Philippines.

SCHOOL POLICY

Today many schools have councils in which young people and their teachers are able to discuss things about their school and come to agreements about some aspects of school life. Does your school have a policy about children's rights? What do you think it should include? When adults have to make decisions about children and young people they are expected to balance what they think a young person needs with what that young person wants. How would you strike that balance yourself? Why not write out your own 'Convention on the Rights of the Child'? What would you include? How would your class or tutor group or year do it? Would things be any different from the way they are now?

The future of human rights

Human rights has come a long way since the English **barons** forced King John to sign the **Magna Carta** in 1215. Gradually, many people have come to accept that people should be treated with equality and allowed to live, in the wonderful phrase of the **United Nations** Convention on the Rights of the Child, 'in the spirit of peace, dignity, tolerance, freedom, equality and solidarity'. Some people do not like to call these things 'rights'. They say that the way we live in society is about balancing our duties and responsibilities. It is true that living together in any group – whether a family, school or nation – involves acting responsibly toward other people. But what if they do not behave responsibly towards you? What if they treat you badly, **abuse** you or prevent you from living with dignity and in peace? It is at times like these that people have in the past turned to language about 'human rights', to defend themselves, to assert their dignity and to establish equality in the place of **oppression** and ill treatment.

But if it is a long road from injustice to equality, it is just as far to go from a verbal commitment to human rights to policies and strategies to make those rights a reality. When the Universal Declaration of Human Rights was re-issued as a booklet in 1998 in celebration of its 50th anniversary, a former **secretary-general** of the UN, Javier Perez de Cuellar, wrote a short introduction in which he reminded us that in 1948 the UN asked all countries to make the Declaration known everywhere but especially 'in schools and other educational institutions'. It was the belief of the writers of the Universal Declaration that if the nations of the world were indeed going to live together 'in the spirit of peace, dignity, tolerance, freedom, equality and solidarity', then we would have to start with the young people of the world.

So if the future of human rights is in the hands of young people, how will young people meet the challenge? All over the world and in many areas of life, there continue to be human rights abuses: in racial discrimination; in wrongful imprisonment; in so-called ethnic cleansing; in the abuse of children or the denial of equal opportunities to women as well as men. Human rights may be seen as an assertion of the dignity of all human beings – the right we all have to equal treatment and equal chances in life, so that we can all share in the good things of the world. But there are still many gaps between the hopeful statements of the many conventions and the realities of life. What can we do to help close those gaps? Look again at the list of internationally recognized human rights on page 29 and of children's rights on page 37. How can we make sure that we live our own lives in the spirit of those rights? What would we have to do to bring the spirit of those rights into our own homes and our own schools?

The future of human rights is in the hands of young people.

CASE STUDY

Experience shows that three types of pressure can make governments change their human rights policies – pressure from:

● other governments
● opposition groups inside the country
● human rights organizations and individuals throughout the world.

We can make a difference!

Timeline

1215 **Magna Carta** .... A step towards equality of treatment in law in England

1642 **Execution of Charles 1** .... The climax of the battle between king and Parliament

1688 **The Bill of Rights** .... A legal arrangement to balance power in England and Wales between king and Parliament. Allowed freedom of speech to MPs

1776 **American Declaration of** .... 'We hold these truths to be self-
Independence evident… that all men are created equal'

1789 **French Declaration of the** .... 'all men are born free and equal in
Rights of Man rights'

1791 **Thomas Paine, *The Rights*** .... Paine thought that despotism runs
of Man through the whole of society leading to oppression of the people

1792 **Mary Wollstonecraft,** .... Called for women to be treated as
A ***Vindication of the Rights*** independent people with their own
of Woman rights

1849 **Henry Thoreau, *Civil*** .... 'that government governs best
Disobedience which governs least'

1859 **J S Mill, *On Liberty*** .... We need to strike a balance between what is right for ourselves and what is right for others

1865 **The Abolition of Slavery in** ...... US president, Abraham Lincoln
the United States called for slaves to be given their freedom after the American Civil War

1946	**Nuremberg war trials**	Nazi leaders on trial for crimes committed during the Second World War
1948	**United Nations' Universal** .... **Declaration of Human Rights**	'All human beings are born free and equal in dignity and rights'
1950	**(European) Convention for** ..... **the Protection of Human Rights and Fundamental Freedoms**	Established the European Court of Human Rights
1955	**Civil Rights Movement** .... **begins in USA**	Protests against segregation laws in United States
1961	**Founding of Amnesty** .... **International**	An organization that monitors and protests against human rights abuses, especially 'prisoners of conscience'
1968	**Assassination of Martin**........... **Luther King**	King was one of the leaders of the Civil Rights Movement
1976	**Race Relations Act**	Outlaws racial discrimination in England, Scotland and Wales
1986	**Sex Discrimination Act**	Outlaws discrimination against men and women in employment, education, services and housing
1989	**United Nations Convention** .... **on the Rights of the Child**	An international treaty to protect children from need and exploitation
1989	**Children Act**	The law which protects children in need in England and Wales
1994	**Nelson Mandela becomes**....... **president of South Africa**	ANC leader that had been imprisoned for 26 years

Glossary

abuse ill-treating someone, especially a vulnerable person

Afrikaans official language of South Africa, spoken mainly by the Afrikaners – descendants of Dutch and other 17th century colonists

apartheid a political system in South Africa which had laws designed to keep black and white communities apart, and to oppress the black community

arbitrary not based on rule or law but on personal beliefs or prejudices

asylum seeker someone who seeks protection in another country from persecution in their own

barbarous brutal or harsh

baron in the Middle Ages, someone who possessed land as a gift from the king. The barons fought for independence against King John, and became powerful landowners in their own right.

campaign a movement organized by people to raise awareness about an issue they care about

civil rights a movement in the US campaigned for civil rights – to give all people equal rights to freedom – for example, to vote, to be educated together, to have equal access to hospitals or other facilities

civil war a war between two or more groups living in the same country

Demopolis Greek term, meaning 'city of the people'

depose to remove someone from their position of authority

diplomacy skilful negotiation to prevent war or to overcome disagreements between different groups or nations

discrimination to treat one person differently from another because of something about them (such as skin colour or choice of sexual partner). Usually the person discriminated against is part of a less-powerful, minority group.

equality of opportunity enabling people from different backgrounds or ethnic groups to have the same chances in life

ethnic concerning any particular racial group or groups. For example, an 'ethnic minority' is a particular racial group who make up only a small part of a whole nation.

exploitation taking unfair advantage of someone

globalization where a product is sold not only in its country of origin, but throughout the world

immigration people moving from their country of origin to settle permanently in another country

imperialism the policy of a government or ruler extending their rule over other territories. It is particularly associated with European governments and the establishment of colonies during the 19th century.

libel a written statement about someone that is untrue

44

Magna Carta the 'Great Charter' – an agreement, signed by King John in 1215, that was the first attempt to limit the powers of the English king and to give everyone the protection of law

media methods by which information is spread – newspapers, radio, television, film and the Internet

merchants people who earn their living by buying and selling

minority small group (less than 50 per cent of the whole)

multi-national corporations businesses whose trade has spread throughout the world and who sell the same products in many different countries

oppression unjust treatment of the weak by the strong

persecution attacking, injuring or even killing someone for their political or religious beliefs

racism the mistaken belief that some races are superior to others

reform/reformer to change something (such as a law or a way of thinking) that is believed to be out of date and unjust; someone who tries to do this is called a reformer

refugee a person who has left their home country because they have been persecuted there and are afraid they will be killed or put in prison

repression using law to oppress a group of people

republic form of government without kings or queens

secretary-general title of the person in charge of an organization such as the United Nations

slander a spoken statement about someone that is untrue

social services sources of help for people in need, provided by the government

social worker someone employed by social services to help the neediest people in society

solicitor lawyer who advises clients on legal matters and prepares legal cases

Star of David symbol of Judaism, consisting of a six-pointed star made up of two equilateral triangles. David was the second king of Israel.

Tyrannopolis Greek term, meaning 'the city of the king'

tyrant ruler who is cruel and unjust

United Nations an association of states that aims to bring about international peace, security and co-operation. Its headquarters are in New York City, USA.

Contacts and helplines

AMNESTY INTERNATIONAL

99-119 Rosebery Avenue
London EC1R 4RE
020 7814 6200
www.amnesty.org
Amnesty International is perhaps the most important group trying to bring pressure on governments to end human rights abuses. Their website is full of up-to-date information about situations in many countries, and gives accounts of particular people who are suffering for their beliefs.

CHILDLINE

0800 111
www.childline.org.uk
a confidential helpline for children

COUNCIL OF EUROPEAN HUMAN RIGHTS

www.dhdirhr.coe.fr

GREENNET

www.gn.apc.org
This is a global computer network designed to link environment, peace, human rights and development groups.

HUMAN RIGHTS

www.4humanrights.com
a portal website that gives you access to many different sites concerned for human rights. For example, it may have information about genocide (the systematic killing of whole nations or races), capital punishment and torture as well as links to pages about left-handedness!

UNITED NATIONS

There are two websites for the UN.
www.un.org
introduces you to the many different aspects of the organization and tell you something of the work the UN does throughout the world
www.unhchr.ch
more particularly about human rights issues as seen by the United Nations. It includes the texts of the Universal Declaration on Human Rights and the Convention on the Rights of the Child.

In Australia

HUMAN RIGHTS AND EQUAL OPPORTUNITIES COMMISSION

Level 8, Piccadilly Tower, GPO Box 5218
Sydney NSW 1042
1300 369 711
www.hreoc.gov.au

AMNESTY INTERNATIONAL AUSTRALIA

GPO Box 1333, Richmond North VIC 3131
www.amnesty.org

AUSTRALIAN RED CROSS

National Resource Centre, 155 Pelham St
Carlton VIC 3053
www.redcross.org.au

COUNCIL FOR ABORIGINAL RECONCILIATION

www.reconciliation.org.au

Further reading

Non-fiction

Britain and the Slave Trade
Rosemary Rees,
Heinemann Educational 1995

Faith in the Poor
Bob Holman
Lion 1998

The Holocaust
Reg Grant
Hodder Wayland 1997

Life Stories: Nelson Mandela
Richard Killeen
Hodder Wayland 1998

Profiles: Adolf Hitler
Richard Tames
Heinemann Library 1998

Profiles: Anne Frank
Richard Tames
Heinemann Library 1998

Profiles: Nelson Mandela
Sean Connolly
Heinemann Library 2000

South Africa during the Years of Apartheid
Rob Sieborger et al
John Murray 1997

The War in Former Yugoslavia
Nathaniel Harris
Hodder Wayland 1997

Fiction

Bring out the Banners
Geoffrey Trease
Walker Books 1995
an account of the fight of women to be given the right to vote at the beginning of the 20th century

Dare to be Different
Elana Bergin et al
Bloomsbury 1999
a collection of stories inspired by the work of Amnesty International

Girl in Red
Gaye Hicyilmag
Orion 2000
the story of a young refugee living on a housing estate

Journey to Jo'burg
Beverley Naidoo
HarperCollins 1996
children travelling in South Africa are brought face to face with the realities of apartheid

Smash!
Robert Swindells
Puffin 1998
a story about the effects of racism

Index